Until the Cardinals Carry Me Home

Until the Cardinals Carry Me Home

M. P. Slaughter

Mermaid Cove Publishing
Gwynn's Island, Virginia

Cover and book design by Angela Clawson, Mermaid Cove Publishing
Author photograph by Tyler Bass, Mr. Ripley's Photography

Publisher's Cataloging-in-Publication
(Provided by Cassidy Cataloguing Services, Inc.)

Names: Slaughter, M. P., author.
Title: Until the cardinals carry me home / M. P. Slaughter.
Description: First edition. | Gwynn, Virginia : Mermaid Cove Publishing, [2025]
Identifiers: LCCN: 2025944240 | ISBN: 9781960430182 (paperback) |
    9781960430199 (ebook) | 9781960430205 (kindle)
Subjects: LCSH: Suicide–Poetry. | Grandmothers–Poetry. | Depression in
    old age–Poetry. | Depression, Mental–Poetry. | Grief–Poetry. |
    Bereavement- -Psychological aspects–Poetry. | Hope–Poetry. | LCGFT:
    Poetry. | BISAC: POETRY / Subjects & Themes / Death, Grief, Loss. |
    POETRY / Women Authors.
Classification: LCC: PS3619.L379 U58 2025 | DDC: 811/.6–dc23

First Edition

Published by Mermaid Cove Publishing,
a division of Mermaid Cove Productions, LLC
PO Box 303, Gwynn, VA 23066
www.mermaidcovepublishing.com

For MawMaw,
You are forever my best friend. I love you.

Contents

The Immediate Aftermath

Struggling While Smiling

Beginnings of Rebuilding

Epilogue

When in eternal lines to time thou grow'st,
So long as men can breathe, or eyes can see,
So long lives this, and this gives life to thee.
-Sonnet #18, William Shakespeare

"It is common folklore that a visit from a cardinal represents a sign from a loved one who has passed. While this belief cannot be traced to a single origin, birds have often symbolized heavenly visitors, messengers to the gods, or even the gods themselves in feathered form."*

*Mayntz, Melissa. "Meaning of the Cardinal: Legends, Lore, and Spiritual Symbolism." Farmers' Almanac, 2024, https://www.farmersalmanac.com/cardinals-legends-lore-and-spiritual-symbolism

Author's Note

One week before Thanksgiving in 2021, my grandmother, Janis Bing Slaughter, lost her life to suicide. She had just turned seventy the month prior and celebrated her birthday surrounded by family and love at one of her favorite restaurants. In the weeks leading up to her death, my grandmother was busy buying Christmas presents and planning our annual Thanksgiving Day lunch.

After her loss, I began seeing cardinals everywhere. Little flashes of red swooped by my vision constantly: in the parking lot ahead of work, on my evening walks with Mollie, at sunset before I could turn in for the night. Cardinals are said to be messengers from the spiritual realm sent by passed loved ones. I like to think that MawMaw was trying to tell me that she would always be with me, even though she wasn't physically here anymore.

I handled my grief like I handle everything else in my life, by writing about it. I missed my grandmother, so I wrote about her. I wrote not only about her death, but also about her life because I did not want to forget all of the good she gave me. I wrote about the depression I suffered that first year because, without her, I did not feel like a whole person anymore. Ultimately, I wrote about surviving.

Until the Cardinals Carry Me Home is a look at how depression and suicide can take anyone at any age, even sweet grandmothers who always seem happy. I wrote this collection as a sort of therapy for myself, as well as a way to show the lasting impacts of suicide on those left behind.

There is always help. There is always hope. However, we must all do better to make that help and hope accessible for everyone.

Come Find Me

Come find me in the forest,
Where I've laid my head to rest
Against a tree that smells so sweet
And implores me to never leave.

I am drunk on the fruit,
I howl with the lone wolves;
And I fear I don't care anymore
That I can't find myself in a mirror.

I sleep in the mouth of a cave,
And ignore what I refuse to brave—
For the dark will still my heart,
Which will never again restart.

The Immediate Aftermath

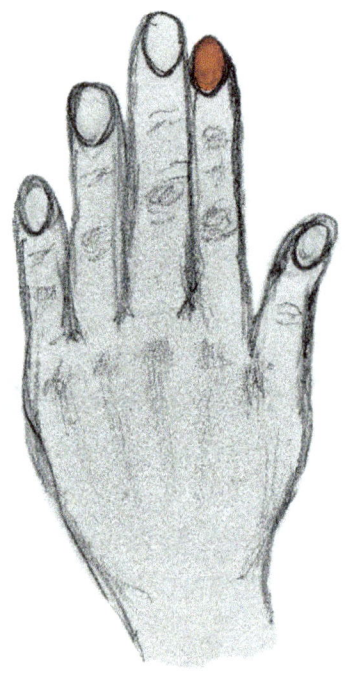

I Paint My Nails **Red** for You

I paint my nails **red** for you,

> Like the cardinal perched atop
> Your hanging snowman feeder;
>
> Like the poinsettia notepad
> You kept stashed in your organ;
>
> Like your favorite coat I gave
> You many Christmases past;
>
> As deep as the wound in your chest,
> Dried-up blood on your blouse;
>
> Like the dress I buried you in
> The day before Thanksgiving;
>
> Like the rust on PawPaw's old
> .38 you held too close—

I paint my nails **red** for you.

What I Said at Your Funeral
(What I wish I said at your funeral)

I am listed as "remarks."
"Janis' granddaughter would like to say a few words."
(These are not "remarks,"
These are not "a few words,"
This is your eulogy).

"My grandmother, MawMaw, was many things in her life:
A talented organist,
A reliable worker,
A dutiful daughter,
A caring wife,
A loving mother,
        grandmother,
        ~~great-grandmother,~~
But, most importantly,
She was my best friend."

The preacher
        Chomps,
                Chomps,
                        Chomps away at his gum.
(You hated to see adults chew gum).

"She always called me her girl,
        Growing up into adulthood.
I was always her best friend,
                her closest confidant,
                and she was mine too.
                        (You still are).

"She meant everything to me.
I'd cry hot, humid tears driving
Back to college after summer
Because I never wanted to be without her.
I'd count down the days until I could see her again."
(I'm counting down the days as I speak).

The preacher smiles like a Sunday afternoon picnic.
(He should not be smiling–show some respect)!

"We'd pluck out tunes on the piano for each other,
    Piano Man, Imagine, Lionel and Lucy;
We'd swap books, crying over *Little Women*
        And poring over the poems of Edgar Allan Poe;
We'd play lots of games, *War, Uno, Old Maid, Monopoly,*
        'There are no friends in Monopoly,'
        Is all she'd say after bankrupting me."

The room is filled to the brim
        With friends
                And family
                        And laughter.
(I'm not trying to be funny. I'm trying to remember you before I forget).

"Growing up, MawMaw played baseball
In the backyard with me and my brother,
        Took us on fishing trips,
        Cared for us when we were sick,
        Made us meals whenever
        We popped by for a sleepover or dinner.
I asked her to make me so many grilled cheeses over the years,
She told me I would turn into one;
At least I was a cheap date, she'd say."

More laughter; I give the room my grayed, tired eyes,
Like the graveyard we have yet to visit.
(I'm not ready for this to be a funny memory yet).

"Celebrating the holidays was always my favorite;
MawMaw just made Christmas so special.
  As soon as Thanksgiving lunch was over, up went the tree,
  Forcing the men to carry the fake fir and all the decorations
  From the trailer to the house every single year,
    With bellies full of turkey and all the fixings.

"We had so many ornaments, we always swore
We would never be able to fit them all on—
We always did, even if the tree
  Leaned a little too much to the left."

I pause for
  More laughter,
    More joy—
      A tear in my heart.
(How am I supposed to do this without you?)

"In the end, it never mattered,
  Just as long as we were all together
    Eating,
      Laughing,
        Enjoying.

"Every moment with MawMaw was special.
  It never mattered what we did
    Or where we went.
      I just wanted to be with her.

"My favorite nights were the ones spent at her house:
Watching the local news,
Then the national news,
Wheel of Fortune,
Jeopardy,
Roseanne or Frasier;

"And stuffing ourselves with
Apple pie,
Pound cake,
Brownies,
Cookies,
Zucchini bread—
Always with a side of vanilla ice cream.

"This routine was so simple,
Comforting,
Familiar,
Solid.

"All my life, she cheered me on:
Sports and school,
My recitals and writings;
I am who I am because of her.
(I don't know who I am without you.)

"My hope is that she continues to be proud of me,
And when she checks in on me from Heaven,
She still says, "That's my girl."

Roaring applause.
A grandstand end.
Words in perfect place.

(What am I supposed to do now?)

After the Funeral

I laughed, I cried,
And now I feel—
Nothing inside.

Your dog and I are
All who are left,
We will remain

Grieved and bereft—
'Til our last days
Our hearts will decay.

Struggling While Smiling

Until the Cardinals Carry Me Home

The cardinal chained to my neck,
Chatters, "This is not your end."

The sun tosses me a wink on our walk
Before setting in a crimson cascade.

I am further from you
Than I was yesterday,
I am closer to you now
Than I will be tomorrow.

I fall to the freezing acrid asphalt,
Bloodying my knees, *who cares*;
Mollie licks at my tears, my fears,
A constant moping mopping.

I will feel sick with loneliness
Until a cardinal appears,
Flying weightless in a sky
Unmarked by storm clouds.

Through my last days, I am doomed to roam,
Until the cardinals carry me home.

Another Way

I think I would have been okay,
If you'd died in any other way:

Illness, accident,
Sudden heart attack;

A cancer diagnosis,
A terminal prognosis.

There was no rushing
To the emergency room;

No paramedic could hope
To resuscitate a hollow home—

You died by your own hand,
That, I cannot bear to stand.

You took from me what was mine,
I will grieve for you all my life.

Fragile

I will shatter under one misplaced word
And fight my enemies from inside my head;

I will cry at an unexpected smile
And hide my true feelings behind one;

I will clench my teeth until my head aches
And scrape my canines against my bloodied lips;

I will eat so much that I feel sick
And resolve to change, but never do;

I will go along with bad ideas
And never sleep the same again;

I will let people who claim to love me hurt me on end
And make them believe I welcomed the pain;

I will desperately cling to this life
And hope the next will be a bit lighter—

I will never not be fragile, like a dripping candle,
And I miss the days when you made me feel whole.

Never the Same

You lost your life to suicide,
But I feel like I also died:

I fell on the pirouette,
I lost in the final set;

I was too focused on me
To remember you have needs.

They tell me there's still beauty in ballets,
And I have yet to be tossed from the game—

But I have not quite righted myself,
Again, only thinking of myself.

Your sun set before I could know,
Now you're buried in the earth below.

I will never be the same,
Without you to lead my way.

I Will Always be Afraid

I will always be afraid, my fears
Will be laid at my grave, so scattered
And frenzied, like an array of dead
Autumnal leaves sticking to my headstone
After a fresh rain—even in death,
My anxieties will still remain.

Trying feels like dying: my twisted stomach
Threatens to erupt, my throat closes
Like an anaphylactic shock—to my system
I am already a walking corpse,
An apparition behind a wall of flesh
And bones—she will not leave me alone!

Waking only to redo the day before
In startling anguish, *nothing is wrong*
If I refuse to tell anyone, my soul
Rots with the limitations of my situation,
Because I was led to water that turned
To blood, and now I am nearly drowned.

A Drinking Solution

I keep sipping the whiskey,
George knows to keep pouring.
I never set down my drink,
The low is too alluring.

Tawnya whispers, "That level
Of crazy in a lady
Intrigues me," to her draining
Weekly dry martini.

I can't stop getting
Drunk off my ass,
I can't stop refilling
My glass; stuck in an echo:

"Self-inflicted gunshot
Wound to the chest."

My anxieties will
Never be laid to rest.

Survive

You survived cancer twice: first in your
Husband's choked-up grave, then
In the blood of your own bones.

You survived your family falling apart like
The flaky crust of an apple pie when first
Cut, the filling oozing out like silent sobs.

You survived partners picking you to
Pieces, like starving seagulls after the
Dried-up remains of an unknowable skull—

But you could not survive all those hours
Living hollow from weathered-down years,
Forgetting hope happens in small moments,
Leaving me to carry the burden to Survive.

Thank Goodness for the Mess

Thank goodness for the mess,
'Cause they'll never notice:
How I pick at my skin
And have gotten so thin;

Stacks of books, scattered clothes,
Piles of plates I loathe;
Hair that tears so easy,
Stomach feels too queasy;

Chipped tables, mismatched chairs,
Pet dander everywhere;
Tight throat, struggled breathing,
Head pounding, dry heaving;

Missing work, focus fades,
I'm just playing charades;
Few missteps, few more beers,
Heartbeat ringing in my ears—

Thank goodness for the mess,
'Cause they'll never notice.

How Could You be Dead?

How could you be dead?
What about when I wed?

I am frenzied—frantic—in an utter panic—

Who will give me my something old,
When I'm stepping into something new;
Who will give me my something borrowed,
When all your flesh is something blue?

Lost relationships, starved for attention:

I am ill on the bathroom floor—
I'm sorry I'm such a chore!

But, my beloved, you are dead,
And take a coffin for a bed.

Why I Write

A written page a day
Keeps the demons at bay;

Sanity's mine to keep
Until I fall asleep;

I can dream tomorrow,
Now I scream my sorrow
'Til the night turns to dawn—
An unbreakable bond,
Like you and I rejoiced—
I'd want no other choice!

Knowing what I know now,
Sweeping grief from my brow,
I'd pick you every time—
You were never not mine.

I know you still love me,
Though you left me at sea
To somehow find a home
I could build as my own.

I write to remember
Every burning ember
Of joy that we once shared—
And to know that you cared.

No
One

No One Cares for a Suicide

No one cares for a suicide,
Pushed aside like pound cake pieces
Baked for post-service fellowship;

Forgotten like cancer patients,
Surrounded by cards and silence
In hospice beds and worn nightwear;

Like mothers who give their families
All, but are left with that creeping emptiness
When no one shows at dinnertime;

As sad as an aging woman whose
Adult children won't fix her birdfeeder—
Willing the cardinals to visit again.

No one cares for a suicide,
But a granddaughter at her desk,
Scratching out her silent screams.

Grandma's Grilled Cheese

There's nothing better than grandma's grilled cheese,
Thick and warm like a hug on Christmas Eve.

Sliced in matching halves, perfectly true,
Like when God cut our soul in two.

Toasted pieces, toughened and blank,
As hardened as I am from heartache.

Gooey yellowed cheddar slipping through,
Messy like my tears when I think of you.

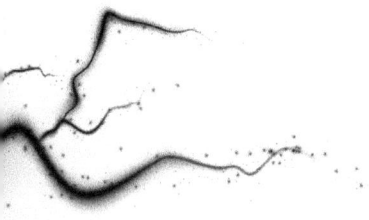

Tell Me When It Ends

Tell me when it ends:
This aching in my chest, weighing me
Down like rain-filled clouds, threatening
To burst into a long-awaited storm.

Tell me when it ends:
This buzzing in my brain, striking like
Lightning, cutting me down as if I'm a fresh
Sapling, just beginning to grow in this world.

Tell me when it ends—
Your sad, pitiful eyes looking back at mine,
Watching me eat the broken shards
Of earth beneath my feet.

I Won't Feel Better

I won't feel better after carefully
Organizing shelves of all my
Favorite books by genre, era,
And subject, doomed to watch my
Collection in better condition than myself.

I won't feel better once I've cleaned
My car of Mollie's winter coat
And all fast food containers, nor dusted
The dashboard and wiped away
The mud from my cracking rims.

I won't feel better making deadline
Every early Wednesday morning,
My fingers tired and sore
From typing all night, sunken
Hollows marring my eyes.

I won't feel better baking
Double chocolate chip cookies
And cleansing the kitchen for my family,
For all my efforts, I'm not present
Enough to appreciate all I give.

I won't feel better Christmas
Shopping several months early,
My Etsy and Amazon lists
So random that the algorithm
Can no longer pin me down.

I won't feel better at the end
Of the day when I've completed
All my work, woven in my ends,
Finished today's chapter, closing
My eyes to live the next tomorrow—

Never will I ever feel better,
Because I'm not getting better.

Stay Strong

"Stay Strong," your last words tucked away
In a copy of "My First Organ Book,"

Back when I tried to be like you,
Back when I thought I could.

But—your talent I could not touch,
Your glow I could not reach.

Your kindness I could not keep,
Your softness—I could never reap.

I Loved You Old

I know you valued being young:

Skating on frozen ponds with your brothers
In socked feet, wary of cracking, splintering ice;

Playing softball on summer days, slowly
Wearing out your catcher's mitt with each pitch;

Loving every bird dog, even before Mollie,
Letting them have the first lick of your ice cream—

But I loved you old:

Smile lines running so deep, I hardly
Believed you spent any time frowning at all:

Mastery over everything from canning
Tomatoes to playing the church pipes;

Not so secretly loving Mollie and I
Above all else, loyal only to us—

You may have missed being young,
But I loved you old.

I Miss You

I miss you when I pick up a new book and
Can only read you between the pages.

I miss you when I window shop and just
Glimpse a glimmer of a ghost in the glare.

I miss you in every sunset, knowing you
Should be enjoying every moment too—

Instead, I'm stuck listening to a dead voice
In the void of a full voicemail box, at a loss.

First Summer

The first summer without you I spent
    Listening to Black Sabbath
        And thinking about dyeing my hair
            Honey blonde with hot pink streaks;

    Licking the salt between my fingers,
        The bay roaring to life in my ears
            And shaking the sand out of my hair,
                Ingrained like my intrusive nightmares;

    Feeling the prickle of spray in my face,
        Salty and sullen, feeling just
            Like my grief in those first months—
                And summer will never be the same.

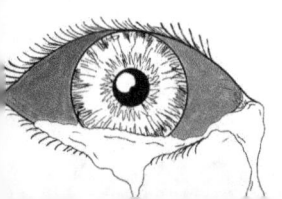

Fine

You were the picture of platitudes,
The definition of a sunny attitude;
A faithful friend, my ride
Or die until the bitter end.

Performing your happy-go-lucky
Disposition, when what you really
Needed was an intervention—

I watched you from the corner of my eye,
And I thought you were Fine, but you proved
Otherwise and now I can't stop crying at night.

Now I pretend I'm Fine, with my pillow
Streaked with tears and my worst fears
Knocking at the door of my nightmares.

Mollie

Mollie holds the heart of my grief—
Soft fur aging and turning white,
Less agile, clumsier every day.

I love her like the puppy she was—
Ten years strong, but growing weaker,
Slowly losing her sharpness after
A life of splashing through summer creeks,
And racing through rows of cucumbers;
The reflection on her collar shining bright,
Like her eyes, when she peered up at you.

Mollie is here now, but not forever,
And I wish I could have been more—
And still be more—for the both of you.

Under Heaven

There's a time and place for everything,

Under Heaven, I have to believe,
Even moments to grieve what you lost
In life, as I grieve what's lost in mine.

I have to believe you're missing me,
Even in paradise up above,
As I'm missing you from down below.

Joined at the hip with Uncle Johnny—
Laughing and playing as kids again,
I have to believe you won't forget

When growing ever-blooming roses—
I have to believe you still notice
All the decay I've been picking through.

Peace is with you, I have to believe,
Or else there'll never be peace with me.

Beginnings of Rebuilding

Church

I never felt like I belonged in a church,
Complete with a steeple and all the people—
And maybe you felt the same all along:

Our communion taken in the form of fried
Chicken stripped from the bone, warm potatoes
Divided into cubes, melting pats of butter;

Our rituals in dealt cards and carefully
Arranged dominoes, Monopoly game
Pieces, strewn about with Scrabble tiles.

I worshipped your organ rendition
Of "In The Garden" and you praised
My advancement with "Amazing Grace."

Did we sin by making our own church?
A place that we called home, a place
Where only you and I were welcome.

Those Men are Not Your Legacy

You were better than the men you fed,
Worth more than the tangled,
Careless sheets, left in a rush,
You straightened on their beds.

Arriving late to plates of labored love,
Thoughtless boot prints tracked on floors,
Eyeing all the yet to be done chores
Crying, screaming for more, more, more—

Your legacy is wrapped in music sheets,
Humming your melodies to pleasant,
Perfect beats, a talent they could only
Dream to score—only left to adore;

Your light I could bask in like early summer
Sunshine, always fresh and freeing—
And that was always more than enough
For your granddaughter, I'll always be.

Coping Mechanisms

Belting pop ballads on my drive home,
Walking Mollie on our rural road;

Vibing to podcasts while making dinner,
Changing into an oversized t-shirt;

Winding smooth yarn around my fingers,
Calming down to Spunky's loving purrs;

Coloring gentle geometric shapes—
Finding ways to take mental breaks.

Cleaning up all our little messes,
Showering until my brain relaxes;

Reading to learn what I don't know,
Playing classical piano notes;

Watching trashy reality T.V.—
Waiting to fall into a dreamy sleep.

"Coward"

I can't stop dreaming
About your suicide,
How quickly the light must
Have left those hazel eyes.

I am hurt every day
By my inattention;
How much you had to say,
In darkness, all alone.

There will be those who whisper,
"Coward," just beyond your grave,
Never knowing how many days
You forced yourself to brave—

That "coward" raised a woman
Who snaps and snarls at whomever
Dares to come after her beloveds,
Any apology vacant from her lips.

I Was Raised by Strong Women

I was raised by strong women,
Never cowering to men,
Holding our family together
With their final ounce of patience
We earned, completely undeserved.

They raised me to be kind and caring,
Always wary, but never weary,
Because I am needed to carry
Our traditions with wrinkling hands,
While wearing a sparkling wedding band.

I keep their life lessons close to heart,
Where they gave me all their love,
Meanwhile, teaching me to be tough
In a world simply not built
For girls of any age, race, or creed—

All men ever raised me to be
Was careful, ever-aware their
Peers were out to desecrate
Us who were not yet able
To consummate a "relationship."

You're Not There

I never visit the cemetery,
Or lay flowers where you're buried.

I can't run my hand over your grave,
Just another tradition taken away—

But you're not there: not in the earth,
Not within the walls of a church;

You're there when I string the tinsel
Through my bright Christmas tree;

You're in every stride I walk,
When I take Mollie around the block.

Your hands guide mine, while I make
The batter for your famous pound cake.

You're there when I desperately need a good book,
And you show me exactly where I need to look—

You're there in every beat I take,
My heart, you will never forsake.

Divine Love

I don't know as much about God
As I once claimed to,
Sitting in Sunday School classrooms

> Learning sin
> Leads to hell
> And hell means
> No more God,
> No more Love.

I don't know whether God is Father
Or Mother, or simply Parent
Who cares in both ways, like you

> Cooking big
> Dinner spreads
> And playing
> Baseball in
> The backyard.

I don't know what mistake I made
To believe God found me unsavable
As a child, drowning in dreamt-up visions of

> Flesh and pained
> Souls with no
> Comforting
> Grandma hugs or
> Gooey grilled cheeses.

I don't know what good I ever did
That God decided to make me yours
For so many years

       Caring for me
       As I could
       Not, letting
       Me breathe in
       Your Divine Love.

I'm Glad I Stayed

I'm glad I stayed,

Through every inappropriate question,
Through every rude insinuation;

Every lost relationship,
Every prolonged hardship.

I'm content with my contempt,
I'm pleased I burned those bridges;

They're not worth all my hate,
They're not worth the space they take.

I'm glad I stayed,

For every smiling face,
For every moment of grace;

All the love I'm not sure I deserve,
All the beauty still left in the world;

Every sunset on a day worth another,
Every breath I could have lost forever—

I will keep living this life,
For myself, and no one else,

I will continue to rebuild my hope,
Until the cardinals carry me home.

Epilogue

Janis Bing Slaughter, 1951-2021

Immortalized

When I have no air left to breathe,
And my time has come to leave—
Decades and decades from now—
You will be enshrined within these
Hallowed pages, your legacy will
Live on even when I cannot.

People can pluck you from shelves
And learn your kindness remains unmatched,
Your talent forever enviable;
How your hope and strength carried
Me through all these years, no matter
How hard certain moments seemed.

Your memory will float through
Thrift stores and e-readers, used
Bookstores and home libraries,
In true immortal form—you will
Never be forgotten or lost to history:
A final gift, fitting for a luminary.

Acknowledgments

I have a lot to be thankful for in my life and I owe my success to the people who have supported me, and continue to support me, even when I know I don't deserve their love and kindness.

I would first like to thank my mother, Tracy Whitehurst, for fostering in me a lifetime love of reading, writing, and learning. She taught me how to read at a very young age and I've had a book in my hand ever since. I owe my college education to her as she was determined to send me, even though money was tight, so I could further develop my writing skills. I would also like to thank her for creating the wonderful illustrations within the pages of this book. My heart is filled with gratitude for you, Mom.

Thank you to my friend, Emma English, who was my very first reader. Your input and friendship have been invaluable through this process, as well as in my life.

Thank you to my fifth grade English Language Arts teacher Marlene Moore who encouraged me to become a writer.

Thank you to Angie and Scott Clawson for giving my words a chance and bringing this project to life. I am so incredibly grateful.

Thank you to Charlie Koenig and Elsa Verbyla who encouraged me to seek publication. Thank you, Charlie for commiserating with me through all of these hard years. Thank you, Elsa for reading about your lifetime friend and classmate through my eyes.

Thank you, Clarence "Huggie" Hargus for taking so many photographs of MawMaw over the years. I cherish them. Thank you for loving us. Thank you for treating me like I'm your own granddaughter.

Thank you to Tricia Miles for giving Mollie, Spunky and myself a home when I had no idea what I was doing with my life. You were so, so kind to us and we will love you forever.

Thank you to Kyle Slaughter for being my big brother and always making sure that my car is in working order, especially when I'm set to go on long trips.

Thank you to my stepfather, Robbie Whitehurst, who is always there when I or anybody else needs him. Thank you for being there for MawMaw whenever she needed her fishing line untangled.

Thank you to Gino Cecchi who wants nothing more than for me to be happy. My heart is yours forever. Thank you to Amanda and Lee Cecchi for wholeheartedly welcoming me into the family.

Thank you to the Bings who have also felt this grief so profoundly. Thank you, Uncle Paul, Aunt Peggy, Aunt Diane, Uncle Roy, Judy, Steve, and Charlene for keeping the family together after our shared tragedy. I am so grateful.

Thank you to my grandmother's very special friends Becky Wilhite and Judy and Jennings Haynes.

Thank you to Mollie for keeping me going in those early days. Without you, I'm not sure where I would be today.

Thank you to my late grandmother, Betty Salmons Hudgins, who also enjoyed writing. I miss you so much.

Thank you to my maternal family for always being there for me. Dawn, Stevie, Cissy Leigh, Donald, Janah, Aaron, Trina, Chris, Aunt Brenda—you rock.

Thank you, Alexia Hopson and André Hopson for always making me feel a part of the family.

Thank you to everyone who was kind to me, even if they had no idea what I was going through. A simple smile and a kind word were so pivotal for me in those early days, I'm not sure if I would have survived without them. I would like to extend a special thank you to Taylor Northrop, Geneva Waynick, Noah Shepherd, Tyler Bass, Lisa Thomas, and Savannah Haugdahl.

I would also like to thank the Randolph-Macon College

English Department for helping me hone my writing skills, particularly Professor Justin Haynes who always pushed me to do better with my poetry.

Thank you to God for creating a place where my grandmother and I can one day reunite.

Lastly, I would like to thank MawMaw. You gave me a lifetime of unconditional love, support, and friendship that I will never be able to pay back. Thank you for being my grandmother and making so many wonderful memories with me. I will miss you until the cardinals carry me home.

www.ingramcontent.com/pod-product-compliance
Lightning Source LLC
Chambersburg PA
CBHW051307140626
46546CB00020B/1284